I0480401

The Great 1929 Stock Market Crash

A Short History

Large Print Edition

By Doug West, Ph.D.

The Great 1929 Stock Market Crash
A Short History
Large Print Edition
By Doug West, Ph.D.
Copyright © 2020 Doug West

All Rights Reserved. No part of this book may be reproduced in any form without written permission from the author. Reviewers may quote brief passages in reviews.

ISBN: 9798656419765

Table of Contents

Preface

Welcome to the book, *The Great 1929 Stock Market Crash: A Short History*. This book is volume 46 of the 30 Minute Book Series and, as the name of the series implies, if you are an average reader this book should take less than an hour to read. Since this short book is not meant to be an all-encompassing history of the 1929 stock market crash, you may want to know more about this dark period in history. To help you with this, there are several good references at the end of this book. I have also provided a Timeline, in order to link together the events leading up to the stock market crash and the aftermath. A section titled "Biographical Sketches" contains brief biographies of some of the key individuals in the book. Thank you for purchasing this book. I hope you enjoy your time reading about the 1929 stock market crash.

Doug West

June 2020

DOUG WEST, Ph.D.

Introduction

The 1920s was a decade of a wonderful ride up for stock market speculators, until it all came crashing down in October 1929. In the course of a few short weeks billions of dollars were lost and thousands of investors were completely wiped out. The explosion of personal debt, low wages, a struggling agricultural industry, overextended speculators, and banks on the verge of insolvency were all factors that helped push the market over the edge. After reaching a peak in early September 1929, stock prices began to decline gradually throughout the month. In October, the pace of the market selloff quickened and panic spread amongst the traders and investors, causing a record drop in the market during the last week of the month. As the market dropped precipitately, investment bankers jumped in to stabilize the market through purchases of large blocks of stock; this caused only a short pause in the avalanche of selling.

After the market reached a crescendo of selling on a day now known as "Black Tuesday," prices of stock stabilized and began to rally for a few months, then the realities of the ensuing depression became clear, driving prices lower. In less than three years the Dow Jones Industrial Average would set the low for the twentieth century, down nearly 90 percent from the September 1929 high. The crash was not the only cause of the Great Depression, but it accelerated the economic convulsions that were felt around the world. By 1933, half of the United States' banks had gone under, and unemployment rapidly approached fifteen million people, which was roughly thirty percent of the working age population.

Reform and relief were attempted by Presidents Herbert Hoover and Franklin D. Roosevelt, which helped to alleviate some of the effects of the market crash and the ongoing depression. But the economy did not make a full turn around until World War II in 1939. It would take twenty-five years before the stock market would once again reach the September 1929 high.

Chapter 1 –
The Roaring Twenties

August 11, 1919 – The Scottish-American industrialist and philanthropist, Andrew Carnegie, dies at age 83. Carnegie led the expansion of the American steel industry in the late 19th century and became one of the richest Americans in history. The Dow Jones Industrial Average closes at 103.94.

The speed at which much of Europe was plunged into war during the late summer of 1914 caught Americans by surprise. The shock of the war threw the financial markets into panic, forcing the closure of the New York Stock Exchange (NYSE) for over four months. The expanding war initially slowed the U.S. economy as trade with Europe was brought to a standstill. As the war progressed the nations of Europe needed food, supplies, and financial support. America stepped into the void to help the beleaguered nations.

President Woodrow Wilson kept America out of the war directly until 1917 when German aggression forced America to enter the war as a combatant on the side of the Allied nations of Great Britain, France, and Russia. The war effort reshaped the American economy, standardizing and centralizing industry as never before. The historian David Noble wrote of the time, "The lesson of the war was that large-scale continuous operation and extensive organized research and development were the essentials of financial success in the chemical industry, and these demanded big companies, corporate organization, and stable markets."

The increase in the demand for products brought runaway inflation, something not seen since the Civil War. Between 1914 and 1920 consumer prices doubled, hurting those on a fixed income. While some suffered from inflation, others prospered; landowners and farmers benefited greatly from rising prices. As the war closed in 1918, the cost of human lives was staggering--the world had lost around 20 million souls. America, in the war less than two years, suffered much less, with 116 thousand dead. Much more devastating than the war was the flu pandemic of 1918, which is estimated to have killed over 50 million worldwide, with nearly 700,000 Americans perishing to the unchecked virus. To punish Germany for its aggressive role in the war, the Allied nations placed very burdensome war reparation payments on Germany, which the war-torn country could hardly repay. Reverberations from the world war, a flu pandemic, rampant inflation, and war reparations would cast a long shadow over the world for the next two decades.

Shortly after the war, America experienced a short-term boom in the economy as manufacturers scrambled to replace inventories depleted by the war effort. Just as quickly as things picked up, the economy rapidly eroded. In mid-1920, wholesale prices began to drop, with farm products and raw material bearing the brunt of the downturn. "What happened," wrote the financial journalist Alexander Nuyes, "was simply that demand for goods by the larger consuming public suddenly stopped...at that moment when the extraordinarily high prices had greatly stimulated supply." The recession that followed lasted through 1921; the stock market lost a quarter of its value, manufacturers cut their workforce by a quarter, half a million farmers lost their homesteads, and 100,000 businesses went bankrupt.

The economic downturn of 1920 and 1921 was short-lived. With the war behind them, people began to spend money again, marking the beginning of the golden age of business and, arguably, the modern age. The Jazz Age, the Roaring Twenties, or simply the 1920s was a booming period of rapid expansion in the economy. Social attitudes were shifting, and society was starting to be less regimented. They were exploring new freedoms, and suddenly the expectations of the people were changing, fueled by the booming economy and new technologies.

Figure – The film actress and dancer Louise Brooks circa 1926. Today she is regarded as a Jazz Age icon and a flapper sex symbol due to the bob hairstyle that she popularized during her career in the 1920s and 1930s.

In the 1920s, economic growth was exceptionally high, leading to a significant increase in living standards. The growing automobile industry, increased consumer confidence, technology improvements, labor productivity improvements, and mass production all helped spur the economy and improve the lives of many

Americans. The Republicans held the majority throughout most of the 1920s in Washington. They favored a laissez-faire approach to business, meaning government had a "hands off" approach to industry. Anti-trust laws were slackened, allowing the growth of monopoly businesses, such as banking. Union membership declined during this time, too. The government offered little legal support for unions, and one of the largest names in auto manufacturing, Henry Ford, banned trades unions at his factories.

With the boost in the economy also came a growth in personal debt. The expansion of advertising in newspapers, magazines, and on radio coaxed the Americans into the stores. The shoppers' desire for the new gadgets knew no bounds and the banks and manufacturers did everything they could to make sure every person could fill their shopping carts, even if it meant monthly installment payments. In 1920, consumer credit spending was $2.6 billion; by the end of the decade it had nearly tripled to $7.1 billion, the largest jump in the history of the country. The editors of *The American Year Book* of 1928 wrote, "[This] plan for merchandising is now recognized as an integral part of our economic life. In short, installment buying has settled down to a more or less normal existence." Journalist Frederick Lewis Allen recalled the period from 1923 to late 1929 as "nearly seven years of unparalleled plenty; nearly seven years during which men and women...believed that at the end of the rainbow there was at least a pot of negotiable legal tender...For nearly seven years the prosperity bandwagon [had] rolled down main street."

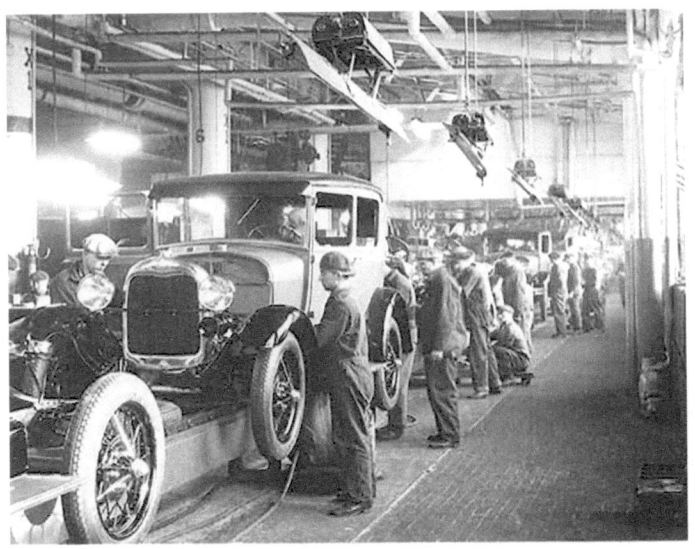

Figure – 1928 Ford Model A assembly line.

During the years from 1922 until 1928, the index of industrial production rose 70 percent, gross national product increased nearly 40 percent, and the per capita income increased by about 30 percent. It was a good time to be an American. The introduction of automation and new technologies greatly increased worker productivity, allowing for a shorter work week and more free time for leisure activities. The soldiers returning from war sparked a housing boom. Along with construction, the automobile industry sprang to life, beginning America's love affair with the automobile. A small-town banker explained the change in people's attitudes, "The paramount ambition of the average man a few years ago was to own a home and have a bank account. The ambition of the same man today is to own a car." This new demand created a boom in the market for cars. As the automaker Walter Chrysler rejoiced, "We were making the first machine of considerable size in the history of the world for which every human being was a potential customer." Men like Chrysler, Henry

Ford, and the head of General Motors (GM) William Durant were leaders in the automobile revolution that may have been the most important new technology since the invention of the printing press.

President Hoover

The enormously popular Secretary of Commerce, Herbert Hoover, won the presidential election of 1928 by a sizeable margin. Hoover started his presidency with a burst of enthusiasm and energy that showcased his progressive political viewpoints. In his inaugural address the new Republican president confidently told a crowd of fifty thousand Americans standing in the rain, "I have no fears for the future of our country. It is bright with hope." Hoover went to work immediately with the assistance of the Republican controlled House and Senate to enact legislation to improve the quality of life of the average American. Hoover's victory was widely perceived as good for the markets and business. The stock market rose in the weeks following the election, with a record number of shares trading hands.

As Secretary of Commerce, Hoover had been critical of the speculative flurry in the market; he worried about the rapid rise in the stock market and even asked for government regulation of banks and stock exchanges to prevent insider trading and margin buying. Secretary Hoover also proposed the Federal Reserve Board raise the interest rates, but the board lowered them, thus fueling the stock market boom that occurred in the two years leading up to his presidency. As a new president, he said nothing to dampen the speculator's enthusiasm.

Chapter 2 –
The Money Men

May 21, 1927 - Charles Lindbergh arrives in Paris after a 33-1/2 hour flight from New York to complete the first solo nonstop transatlantic flight. The Dow Jones Industrial Average closed at 172.06.

Banking had changed little since the late nineteenth century, dominated by large institutional banks. This all began to change in the 1920s, when banks began to offer a variety of products and services, becoming virtual "financial department stores." As part of this process, commercial banks were moving into the securities business despite the vague constraints imposed on them by the National Banking Act passed during the Civil War. The banks saw expansion into brokerage services and underwriting of bonds as a natural extension of their business. Many antiquated laws prohibited the banks from expanding; most states prohibited commercial banks from crossing state lines to open a branch in an adjacent state, and other laws limited the expansion within its own state. As the country and the economy sprang forward, banks were constrained, limiting their ability to make money and create credit. The laws did allow commercial banks to open subsidiary companies across state lines. The bank of J.P. Morgan had its subsidiary Drexel in Philadelphia and other large banks followed suit, establishing subsidiaries in distant cities.

After World War I, the demand for credit was more than the small banks and credit companies could handle. Competing for the available credit were the stockbrokers looking for margin money to loan to their clients for market speculation. The speculators who did not have enough money to buy a sizeable position in the stock market borrowed money from the brokers, called "margin." It was common practice to put down as little as 10 percent of the value of the stock to be purchased, with the other 90 percent being financed by the broker at a high interest rate. The margin money allowed the small customers to greatly expand their stock purchases; however, it also greatly increased their risk if the price of the stock dropped. The loans to stockbrokers, though riskier than mortgage loans, paid the lenders nearly twice the interest rate, making it very lucrative. The high demand for credit led to loan sharking, especially in urban areas. As well as making bootleg liquor for the thirsty masses during the Prohibition years, organized crime moved into the loan sharking business. To little effect, states began passing usury laws to limit the exorbitant interest rates charged by the loan sharks.

Charles Mitchell, the head of New York's National City Bank, was a prominent figure in the race to sell the average Americans stocks and bonds. As the disposable income of men and women rose during the 1920s, they had money in their savings accounts that needed to be invested profitably.

The bond drives during World War I to finance the war effort had introduced the general public to the idea of purchasing securities, in this case bonds, as a way to save their money and build wealth. Men like Mitchell and thousands like him were there to sell the working men and women stocks and bonds as a path to wealth. The National City Company used the bank's extensive client lists to expand their selling of securities to new customers previously untouched by traditional brokerage houses. During the first half of the 1920s, bonds were the security of choice hawked by the brokers. As the decade wore on, the more volatile and potentially more profitable stocks became the favorite product of the salesmen.

Figure – (Left to right) Charles E. Mitchel, William C. Durant, and Joseph P. Kennedy.

The National City Company set the mold for the one-stop financial department store, a model that would endure for decades. With branches and subsidiaries in fifty cities, National City was able to offer their customers a branch bank (where it was allowed), a securities office, and a trust office to prepare wills and administer estates. Mitchell hired hundreds of financial salesmen to reach out to prospective customers. In Mitchell's training classes he told the new recruits, "Our branch offices throughout the United States are already working to make connections with the great new bond buying public...and are preparing to serve the public on a straightforward basis, just as it is served by the United Cigar Stores or Child's Restaurant." During a noontime sales luncheon, Mitchell told his team of 350 salesmen dining at the Bankers Club in Manhattan, "There are six million people with incomes that aggregate to thousands of millions of dollars. They are just wanting for someone to come and tell them what to do with their savings. Take a good look, eat a good lunch, and then go down and sell them." The boss made sure everyone understood: sell securities or look for a new job.

The bank took full advantage of the burgeoning advertising business, spending on lavish newspaper and magazine advertisements touting their many financial products. National City tried to maintain a professional image by educating their customers about stocks and bonds through slick informative pamphlets. By the late 1920s National City had become one of the largest underwriters of bonds, issuing between $1 and

$2 billion per year. National City Company became a financial behemoth with almost two thousand employees and sixty branches in more than fifty cities.

Bonds, however, with their fixed interest rate and low volatility, didn't appeal to the speculators seeking to get rich. Buying and selling stock was the ticket to wealth and brokers did everything they could to fuel the frenzy. The media played its role with tales of traders accumulating vast fortunes in a relatively short period of time. The press became a tool of the large speculators, and clandestinely the market manipulators put many well-known journalists on their payrolls. A timely article touting a company by a respected business journalist did much to bolster the price of a stock. Since the ownership of stocks by the general public was a relatively new development, they were ignorant of the shark infested waters in which they swam, and the professional traders took full advantage of their naivete. Other giants in the realm of market speculation were Jesse

Livermore, Joseph P. Kennedy, and Bernard Baruch. Men like these and many others became legends in the financial community and were envied by those who sought to emulate their success.

For anyone making a lot of money, paying the tax bill has always been a problem, and the traders of the 1920s were no exception. At that time tax rates were as high as 70 percent in the top brackets. Clever stock speculators developed a method known as a "wash sale" to avoid paying taxes on their profits. In a wash sale one individual would sell a stock to another individual at an artificially low price, claiming the loss as a tax deduction. Traders would normally arrange a wash sale with a family member, usually their wives, turning a profit into a tax loss in the eyes of the Internal Revenue Service.

The stock bull market—a period of rising prices--turned into a raging stampede in 1927 when the Comptroller of the Currency, authorized under provisions of the McFadden Act, was given the power to allow banks to underwrite securities. Up until this time, most stock underwriting and trading was the province of investment banks like J.P. Morgan. The commercial banks were forbidden from underwriting stock and were relegated to the issuance of bonds. As result of the new law, the issuance of the number of stocks skyrocketed and so did the market itself. Between 1926 and 1928 the number of new stocks increased by eight-fold, while there was little change in corporate bond issuance. As a result, loans made to brokers for margin money by companies other than banks tripled, while the index of common stock doubled. The comptrollers' decision boosted the stock market, leading Charles Mitchell to proclaim that stocks had a place in every investor's portfolio, because, according to him, they were "as safe as bonds."

Investment Pools

With the lack of regulation over stock trading, shrewd traders took advantage of the many loopholes in the regulations and developed strategies that netted large profits. Investment pools were formed by wealthy traders and speculators for the purpose of market manipulation; pushing a stock price higher or lower. Unless the pool consisted of traders already working on the stock exchange floor, an investment pool needed a floor trader to execute their trades, which they were glad to do for a price. At its essence, a pool was a hastily assembled organization existing solely for the purpose of manipulating the price of a stock.

A celebrated trader who helped run up the market before the crash was William "Billy" C. Durant. A short, dapper man, Durant was one of the founding fathers of General Motors. When he lost control of GM he moved into stock speculation in a big way. Durant assembled a syndicate or pool of wealthy investors, who reportedly bought and sold over $4 billion of common stock. Durant's pool of investors had become a common method for the wealthy investor to speculate in the market. The pools would use a "pump and dump" strategy to make fantastic profits. With the help of favorable press reports on a company, which often was bought and paid for by the pool, the ring of speculators piled into a stock, forcing the price to rise dramatically. As the general public saw the price rise they bought into the stock; all the time the public was buying at the elevated prices, the pool speculators were selling into the hysteria, netting a handsome profit while the average investor lost money when the stock price collapsed. It is estimated that Durant made $50 million in three months by speculating prior to the crash.

One of the best-known investment pools of the 1920s was for Radio Corporation of America (RCA), known simply as Radio. The RCA stock specialist on the trading floor of the New York Stock Exchange was the wealthy and experienced Michael Meehan. Meehan felt Radio stock was too low and was ripe for manipulation. With his connections he was able to openly establish a pool of more than $12 million. Some of the notables in the pool were John Raskob, builder of the Empire State Building, who contributed $1 million; the auto magnate Walter Chrysler, who subscribed for $500,000; Billy Durant was in for $400,000; and Meechan, through his wife, invested $1 million.

Aided by a couple of favorable newspaper articles about RCA the stock price began to move from $81 to $92. The pool kept buying until the price reached $100, then they began to sell their position to the hungry investors looking to profit. The pool netted $5 million in profits for their efforts, while other investors who had sold Radio short at lower prices suffered significant loses. Just as quickly as the pool was formed, it was dissolved. To avoid any hint of impropriety, like Meehan, the other floor traders in the pool used the names of their wives as investors.

Chapter 3 – The Stock Market Rises, The Economy Falters

December 2, 1927 – The Ford Motor Company introduces the new Model A automobile, successor to the venerable Model T. Within two years over 1 million Model As have been sold. The Dow Jones Industrial Average closes at 196.75.

By the end of the 1920s America had become a tale of two worlds–the stock market kept going up for some unseen reason, yet the average family began to feel the pinch from low wages, too much debt, and low farm prices. By the end of the decade the production capacity of the factories had outpaced demand by an estimated 17 percent; in short, there were many more goods available than there were buyers. Realizing a shortfall in sales, the manufacturers cut back on production, and as inventory levels grew, wholesale prices fell. The humorist Will Rogers asked in a newspaper column in 1932: "Gosh, wasn't we crazy there for a while? Did the thought ever enter our bone head that the time might come when nobody would want all these things we're making?"

Some economic historians believe the lack of demand from products may have been a result of a dip in the population of the men and women in their thirties and forties, their prime years for earning and spending. The dip was probably a result of the millions who died worldwide from World War I and the more deadly 1918 Spanish flu pandemic. This was manifest in the decline in nonfarm households during the twenties. Shortly after World War I there was a brief housing boom as soldiers returned from the war and began to establish families. After the initial boom, construction of residential homes began to slow. In 1925 the amount spent on new homes was over five billion dollars, and by 1933 the amount had dropped dramatically to less than half a billion dollars. Economic historian Clarence L. Barber has claimed: "Thus the rapid and very large decline in the rate of growth of nonfarm households was clearly the major reason for the decline that occurred in residential construction in the United States from 1926 on. And this decline...may well have been the most important single factor in turning the 1929 downturn into a major depression."

Farmers suffered largely during the 1920s while their incomes shrank to only a third of the national average. The chief problem was overproduction. They benefited from the new technologies that increased their productivity, but a large amount of production, along with competition from overseas, caused the prices at the market to drop dramatically. By the time Herbert Hoover became president in early 1929, the agricultural sector was already failing. The president opposed subsidies, as did his congressional allies; instead, he supported a bill that created the Federal Farm Board. With a $500 million budget, the farm board loaned money to farmers to make and strengthen farm cooperatives in the hope that they would control production and bring the crops to market in a more efficient manner. In June of 1929, Congress passed the Agricultural Marketing Act, complete with the Federal Farm Board and no subsidies. Hoover obtained his agricultural program but not without a significant cost politically.

Another factor hurting the farmers and manufacturers was the tight credit market, making the purchase of new equipment and land very expensive. The demand for money for investment in the stock market was driving competition for the available credit, forcing up loan interest rates. The senator from Iowa, Smith Brookhart, told the Senate that "borrowed money will cost the farmer more in 1929 than it did in 1928, due to the high money rates enforced by the phenomenal industrial expansion and stock market turnover in the last five years."

Figure - A U.S. farmer listening to a crystal radio set around 1922. The crystal radio, which didn't require electricity to operate, was ideal for farmers to keep updated on the weather and agricultural prices.

***

The speculative run-up in the stock market had many naysayers who issued warnings that the boom would soon end. In January 1925, Senator Henrick Shipstead of Minnesota spoke out against the loose money polices of the Federal Reserve, stating: "[T]he greatest menace which I see in the present situation is the effect upon [a] hundred million minds...when it at last dawns upon the common man...that our boasted national prosperity hangs, not upon the productive industry and wage earnings toil but upon the use of government financial functions in aiding the stock market operations." Shipstead and his colleagues were not the only ones concerned about the growing stock market bubble. The heavyweight financier Paul M. Warburg, who had helped write the legislation that created the Federal Reserve system in 1913 and had served on the first Federal Reserve Board, was critical of the stock market and the board of the Federal Reserve. In March 1929, Warburg wrote, "If orgies of unrestrained speculation are permitted to spread too far... the ultimate collapse is certain not only to affect speculators themselves, but also to bring about a general depression involving the entire country." Little did he realize when he wrote those words how prophetic they would soon become. Warburg was immediately harangued by his Wall Street brethren, who accused him of "sandbagging American prosperity." Following his own advice, he pulled out of the stock market, suffering little loss when the crash finally came.

As the excitement built around the rising market, people traveled, some from great distances, to be a part of the action. The financial district had become New York City's main tourist attraction. The crowds outside the financial institutions cheered the Wall Street personalities as they arrived for work in the morning. Just as the big players in the financial district were becoming minor celebrities, cracks were beginning to appear in the wall of money that propped up the frothing market. In March of 1929, the stock market saw the first major reversal. This mini panic was upended by a strong rebound that summer. However, by October, most shares were highly overvalued and when some companies posted the disappointing results of their profits, many investors felt it was a good time to cash in on their shares. The crash had subtly begun.

Chapter 4 – The October 1929 Stock Market Crash

November 29, 1929 – Commander Richard E. Byrd and three companions return to their home base at Little America in the Antarctic after completing the first flight over the South Pole. The Dow Jones Industrial Average closes at 238.95.

Theories abound on what caused the stock market to crash in late 1929. Some favor the explanation that the stock market crash was brought on by the country's weakening economic conditions, a shoddy banking system, easy credit, and the lack of regulation of the markets. Others prefer to believe the problem was a result of forces in Europe that had perverted the market. The economic historian Charles R. Geisst lays the crash and the start of the depression squarely at the feet of Wall Street, writing: "Wall Street itself was primarily responsible for the crash and subsequent depression...Wall Street and the banking community were directly responsible for economic conditions as October 1929 approached. Any suggestion that they merely reflected the general state of the economy ignores their enormous effect on the cost of money and human behavior in general."

The large operators on Wall Street realized the lofty valuations of stocks couldn't last and began to liquidate their positions. Joseph Kennedy started closing out his holdings in 1928. The March 1929 "break" in the stock prices with record volume gave a clue to many of the major speculators such as Bernard Baruch, John Roskob, and others that it was time to begin selling their shares. Baruch offered insight after the crash as to why he had gone through the crash relatively unscathed: "Repeatedly in my market operations I have sold stock while it was rising. And that has been one reason why I have held on to my fortune." The warning signs were there in the form of extended price-to-earnings ratios, normally in the range of 10 to 50. The Alleghany

Corporation had a price-to-earnings ratio of 108, Columbian Gramophone's was 129, Cities Service's was 165, and National City Bank's was 120. The market remained unphased as volume of stocks trading on the NYSE held steady around the average of four million shares trading hands per day throughout the winter and spring of 1929. Toward the end of March 1929, Charles Mitchell of the National City Bank of New York defied Hoover's request for bankers to limit credit for stock speculation and offered ready loans for the purchase of stock. Senator Carter Glass, chairman of the Senate Banking Committee, denounced Mitchell's action. In April, Hoover requested that editors and publishers of newspapers campaign against speculation–few complied.

Figure – Closing prices for the Dow Jones Industrial Average from beginning of 1920 to the end of 1939.

On August 8, the Federal Reserve Bank of New York increased its discount rate an entire percent, from five to six percent. On September 26, the Bank of England raised the discount rate one percent in order to slow the flow of gold from England into the U.S. stock market. Both upward moves in the interest rate put a damper on the amount of new money flowing into the stock market. In early October, prices of stocks began to slide as the lofty valuations were no longer sustainable. On October 4, the heading of the *New York Times* was titled "Year's Worst Break Hits Stock Market." The *Times* article cited reasons for the stock prices decline: a larger broker loan was expected, weakening margin accounts were making it necessary to sell, and possibly the most troubling was a statement made by Philip Snowden, England's Chancellor of the Exchequer, who described America's stock market as a "speculative orgy." The Snowden statement carried weight and was also mentioned in a *Wall Street Journal* article.

At the end of trading on Wednesday, October 16, stock prices were down. The next day's headline of the *Washington Post* told the story with the headline "Crushing Blow Again Dealt Stock Market." The front page article stated, "The index of 20 leading public utilities computed for the Associated Press by the Standard Statistics Co. dropped 19.7 points to 302.4, which contrasts with the year's high established less than a month ago..." The *Post* articles were important because they were Associated Press (AP) releases, with a wide audience in newspapers across the nation. The *New York Times* reported on the 17th that the utility stocks had suffered most in the day's break. On October 19th, the *Washington Post* headline was "20 Utility Stocks Hit New Low Mark."

On Monday, October 21, the market fell again. The causes identified by news outlets were margin sellers, short selling, and foreign money liquidation. A short seller believes a stock or commodity will drop in price. To profit from the drop, the short seller borrows the shares, for a fee, from the broker and sells the shares into the market. After the stock price drops, the short seller buys the stock back from the market and replaces the borrowed stock. The seller profits the difference between the higher price at which he sells the stock and the lower price at which he buys back in. A short seller loses money if the price of the stock rises, forcing the short seller to buy back the stock at a higher price.

On Wednesday, October 23, panic selling set in. The *New York Times* reported "Prices of Stocks Crash in Heavy Liquidation" and the *Washington Post* reported "Huge Selling Wave Creates Near-Panic as Stocks Collapse." In a market valued at $87 billion dollars, $4 billion dollars were lost, nearly a five percent drop. The economic reporter Matthew Josephson wrote of that Wednesday: "I heard—and I can still hear it—the sound of running feet, the sound of fear, as people hastened to reach posts of observation before the gong rang for the opening of trading. Hypnotized by their panic, the crowds in the boardrooms stared in horror at the stockboards or the tape recording their progressive ruin."

On a day that is now called "Black Thursday," October 24, the stock market traded a record number of 12,894,650 shares, which was three times a normal day's volume. The previous record had been 8,246,742 on March 26 of the same year. The trading floor was shut down for lunch, when a hastily convened meeting of the nation's top bankers took place at the House of Morgan at 20 Wall Street. After the meeting, Thomas W. Lamont, the head of the House of Morgan, held a short press conference. To restore some order to the chaos, he calmly addressed the reporters, "There has been a little distress selling on the stock exchange...and we have had a meeting of the heads of several financial institutions to discuss the situation." The bankers had decided to make massive purchases in the market to assuage the fears of the traders. That afternoon the president of the Exchange marched out onto the trading floor and started purchasing large blocks of the key stocks: U.S. Steel, RCA, General Motors, AT&T, and others. The dumping of twenty to thirty million dollars into the market worked; prices rose at least for the day. The stock tickers that reported the stock price to the rest of the world were hours behind as the sales volume was too high to record all the trades. When a trader dumped their stock at the peak of the panic, it would be hours later before they knew the exact price that the stock sold for.

Treasury officials blamed the speculation on the news. The *New York Times* blamed the cost of call money being twenty percent in March and the price break in March being understandable, but the call money in October was only five percent. Call loans are a loan payable on the demand of the lender. There shouldn't have been a crash, according to the *New York Times*. The *Wall Street Journal* released an article giving the New York bankers credit for stopping the price decline with their massive buying support.

Figure - A solemn crowd gathers outside
the New York Stock Exchange after the crash in 1929.

But Black Thursday was not the end of the fall, rather an opening act for the main event. On Monday October 28, there were another 9,212,800 shares traded; three million of those were in the final hour when the market dropped nearly 13 percent, making it the third worst day in the complete history of the Dow Jones Industrial Average. The following Tuesday, October 29, has become known as "Black

Tuesday" for the high down volume and the nearly 12 percent drop in prices. The headline in the next day's edition of the *Times* was "Stocks Collapse in 16,410,030 Share Day." RCA lost nearly a third of its value that day, while U.S. Steel lost about 15 percent. As word spread throughout the financial district of New York, crowds began to form in front of the Exchange building. Soon there were ten thousand wandering the streets in stunned amazement. Some turned to religion and found solace by quietly sitting in the pews of the nearby Trinity Church. By the end of the day, all the gains of the bull market of 1929 had been erased, leaving thousands of investors in ruins. The stock market lost almost $16 billion dollars in the month of October, and 29 public utilities had lost over $5 billion dollars that month, by far the largest loss of any industry tracked by the *Times*.

Chapter 5 – The Beginning of the Great Depression

July 14, 1931 – An acute financial crisis forces all banks in Germany to close. The value of the German Mark drops and the country is on the verge of insolvency. The Dow Jones Industrial Average closes at 140.85.

The stock market crash left an indelible image in the minds of the American public. Gone was trust in markets, bankers, and politicians. The once heralded titans of Wall Street became despised men of greed and avarice. The crash didn't spell the end of Wall Street, but it did cause dissension within the ranks. Those at the bottom of the financial pyramid, the traders and speculators, realized they had also been duped by the powerful investment bankers in the corner offices who had withheld valuable information. As 1929 turned into 1930 the number of new stock issues dropped appreciably, and capital investment in industry diminished.

In November and December of 1929, the government took decisive action to prevent the economy from slowing further. President Hoover announced a one percent tax cut, intended to put more money in the pockets of lower income families. To stimulate the nation's financial system the Federal Reserve began dropping interest rates. As the financial crisis worsened, Congress and the public sought someone to blame for the country's economic woes.

President Hoover's actions in the wake of the stock market crash were based on his belief that the economy faced a downturn rather than a complete collapse. His actions accorded with his faith in cooperation, voluntarism, and the value of statistics and expertise. President Hoover reacted to the crash of the stock market and the oncoming economic downturn by meeting with major industrialists in a series of conferences. Some of the notable figures present at the meetings were Thomas Lamont and George Whitney of J.P. Morgan, Albert Wiggin of Chase,

Henry Ford of Ford Motor Company, and Charles Mitchell of National City. Hoover let it be known that maintaining public optimism in the coming months was paramount. Privately he told the businessmen that he feared the nation's economy was on the verge of collapse and their cooperation was necessary to avoid a general depression. Most of the business leaders promised to continue to invest in their industries and not reduce wages. Henry Ford went so far as to promise to raise wages to $7 per day and increase his investments by $30 million in 1930. The president of the National Electric Light Association promised Hoover that the members would commit to increasing their investment by $110 million over the next year. Apparently, the message of optimism by Hoover and the business leaders influenced the investing public, for by the end of 1929 the stock market was beginning to show signs of recovery. The renewal of the market continued into the spring. Politicians continued the cheery rhetoric and Secretary of Commerce William Doak explained, "Normal business conditions should be restored in two or three months." In June, analyst Merryle Rukeyser wrote glowingly of Hoover, "I am one of those who thinks that the engineer in the White House made a magnificent gesture to stem psychological panic and to demonstrate that the human will could be an effective contributing cause in shaping the course of the business cycle."

Despite the glowing rhetoric the true picture was less than rosy. Few of the promises the industrialists had made to Hoover came to fruition. The numbers told the true story: Between the end of 1929 and the end of 1930, gross domestic investment by the private sector declined from $35 billion to $23.6 billion and would be less than $4 billion by the end of 1932. The promises made by Henry Ford did not ring true; the $7 per day wage only become a reality in 1931, nearly two years after the meeting with Hoover. The dark side was that Ford fired thousands of his workers and subcontracted much of Ford's work out to independent companies that paid as low as 12.5 cents an hour.

Figure – Unemployed men standing in line outside a depression era soup kitchen in Chicago.

By the middle of 1930 earnings were starting to be reported by the corporations and it was a distressing picture. The National City Bank issued the results of their survey of two hundred companies, which showed an average decline of 19 percent. The transportation industry took the brunt of the hit, reporting automobile companies showing a 40 percent drop, with the railroads showing similar damage. There were some bright spots; the fields of advertising, radio, and motion pictures had increased profits in 1930. It would not be until nearly three full years after the crash that the market would reach its low point. The Dow Jones Industrial Average closed at 41 on July 8, 1932, a low for the twentieth century.

Though only a small percentage of Americans owned stock directly, the impact of the crash rippled through the nation and the people looked to the government to help during this troubling time. President Hoover, a man of the numbers, ordered the Department of Labor and Commerce to come up with a precise and accurate economic statistics report. To his dismay, the report showed that in the week and a half before Christmas Day of 1929, one million Americans had lost their jobs.

Hawley-Smoot Tariff

Most today believe the stock market crash of 1929 was not the cause of the Great Depression; it is viewed more as a symptom rather than a cause. Much of the blame for transforming an economic downturn into a depression has been associated with the Hawley-Smoot Tariff signed into law by President Hoover on June 17, 1930. The tariff was designed to support prices for farmers and maintain employment. President Hoover faced stringent objections from the financial circles, and 1,028 academic economists signed a petition against it. Thomas Lamont of the House of Morgan later said, "I almost went down on my knees to beg Herbert Hoover to veto the asinine Hawley-Smoot Tariff. That Act intensified nationalism all over the world." The tariffs imposed by the act on hundreds of products sparked an international trade war. As a result, the volume of world trade shrank by two-thirds from the last quarter in 1929 to the first quarter in 1933. Whether the Hawley-Smoot Tariff was the leading cause of the Great Depression or not, it has been demonized throughout the succeeding decades. According to Jude Wanniski, a prominent supply side economist during the Reagan and Carter years,

"The stock market crash of 1929 and the Great Depression ensued because of the passage of the Smoot-Hawley Tariff Act of 1930." Richard Cooper, who served as undersecretary of state under President Carter gave a bleaker view of the tariff, writing, "The seeds of the Second World War, both in the Far East and Europe, were sown by Hoover's signing of the Hawley-Smoot Tariff."

President Hoover continued to struggle throughout the remainder of 1930 and 1931 to break the depression. He called for more federal assistance by noting that, "We used such emergency powers to win the war, we can use them to fight the Depression, the misery and suffering from which are equally great." However, none of the programs or reforms initiated by the Hoover administration appeared to be working—the nation's finances were sinking into the abyss and dragging other countries of the world down with America. The political firestorm that was created by the depression and the failure of his policies caused the president and the Republican Party significant political damage which the electorate would make clear in the coming election of 1932.

Reconstruction Finance Corporation

To help resurrect the economy President Hoover called upon the nation's leading bankers to each contribute $25 million to establish a national credit pool to bail out areas of the economy in trouble. Called the National Credit Corporation, it failed to receive support from the bankers, as unsecured loans to failing companies were not good for their bottom line. Hoover, disappointed with the banker's disinterest, prompted Congress to create the Reconstruction Finance Corporation (RFC). The government run and funded agency was meant to stabilize the financial structure of the nation through providing credit to banks that were both weak and strong, as well as other entities like agricultural organizations and railroad construction. The president hoped that by improving the financial health of the nation, public confidence would be boosted, and employment opportunities and international trade would grow. Congress created the RFC in the early months of 1932. Originally the RFC was funded with $500 million and was meant to make loans to troubled banks, financial institutions, and other industries in need of credit. One problem that plagued the organization and hampered its effectiveness was the public nature of the list of banks and organizations in trouble. Once short sellers smelled trouble, they began to sell the stock, driving down the share price. Scared depositors would demand their money, causing a run on the banks. The loans became more discrete to avoid the unintended negative consequences. The issue became political, and the Democratic Speaker of the House, John Nance Garner, reversed his position, making the list of troubled banks public, forcing many banks into failure. Partisan politics hampered the role of the RFC until Franklin Roosevelt became president and the House and Senate both came under Democratic control. Under Roosevelt New Deal policies, the powers of the RFC were expanded to offer support to other types of businesses. However, banks were still hesitant to request loans to avoid a run on their bank. The RFC existed until 1957 when it was felt that it was no longer needed.

Bank of United States Failure

The fragile banking system was one of the leading culprits that caused much of the economic mayhem of the 1920s and 1930s. The banks suffered from poor regulation, inept management, and a proclivity for irresponsible investments, such as California and Florida real estate speculation. At the end of December 1930, the single largest bank failure occurred when the United States Bank along with its $300 million in deposits went under. Regardless of the official sounding name, Bank of United States (note *the* is purposefully missing), was simply a local New York bank which had been taking advantage of, primarily, the immigrants who worked in the garment district. One depositor remembered the day the bank closed, "It was a terrible time...You felt as though the bottom had dropped out of your life, and I guess the thing that bothered me most was the fact that there had been no notice." The failure of the Bank of United States was the largest bank failure in America up until that point in history. It was also a harbinger of more pain to come.

Figure – A crowd of depositors gathered in the rain outside Bank of United States after its failure in 1931.

In the election of 1932 Hoover was soundly defeated by Democrat Franklin D. Roosevelt. Hoover had come into office during the peak of the 1920s' economic prosperity and left office as the president who, deservedly or not, was blamed for the stock market crash and the start of the Great Depression. Roosevelt swept into office with an assortment of plans to revive the economy he called the "New Deal." They were voted into action by Congress during President Roosevelt's first term. The New Deal began a political realignment that positioned the Democratic Party as the new majority. The party based their platform on promising improvements in the factories within the cities, expanding liberal beliefs, empowering labor unions, and supporting minorities. There were some Republicans who supported Roosevelt's programs, but most were in opposition, claiming the programs were socialistic, destructive to business, and hampered private investment.

Chapter 6 –
The Regulation of Wall Street

November 3, 1936 – Franklin D. Roosevelt is reelected president of the United States by a landslide over Republican opponent Alfred M. Landon. The election proves to be an overwhelming endorsement of Roosevelt's New Deal policies. The Dow Jones Industrial Average closes at 176.67.

As the stock market had its meteoritic rise during the 1920s, just the opposite was true in the 1930s. During the glory days of the market boom, investment bankers, brokers, and the major traders became the new celebrities. After the crash, they gained the moniker "banksters," akin to gangsters. With this fall from grace, the public demanded satisfaction and politicians were more than happy to redeem themselves and demonize the very men they once idolized.

President Hoover, opposed to the practice of short selling, in 1931 revived his interest in stopping the practice that was destroying the economy, commenting, "Individuals who use the facilities of the Exchange for such purposes are not contributing to the recovery of the United States." His position was endorsed by many business leaders, fearing their stock could be the object of short sellers. In 1932 Hoover threatened the NYSE with regulation if they did not end the practice, but little change occurred and the practice continued. The president also requested commodity futures exchanges to discourage short sellers in order to pump up the price of farm commodities.

In March 1932, the Senate Committee on Banking and Currency launched an investigation of the market crash of 1929. Members of the Democratic party criticized the investigation, claiming it was simply a ploy by the Republicans to placate Americans who had lost money in the market. For the first eleven months the committee made little progress. Their efforts were thwarted by bank executives who repeatedly denied requests for records and internal documents. In early 1933, the committee hired a new chief council, the former New York deputy district attorney Ferdinand Pecora. Pecora was aggressive in his new role and subpoenaed high-profile bankers to testify, realizing their appearance before the committee would generate significant press coverage.

One of the titans of industry brought before the committee was the chairman of National City Bank, Charley "Sunshine" Mitchell. To prepare for the bankers' appearances, Pecora subpoenaed internal bank documents. He and his staff sifted through the piles of paper looking for evidence of wrongdoing. The committee selected Mitchell because he was the head of the nation's second largest bank and, according to the committee chairman Peter Norbeck, "its [National City] recognized leadership in the orgy of speculation which led to the business collapse." Through

Pecora's skill as a prosecutor he was able to elicit confessions from Mitchell that severely damaged his reputation. In testimony, Mitchell admitted that in 1929 his salary and bonuses amounted to over $1.2 million, and he acknowledged selling National City stock to a family member at a considerable loss to avoid paying taxes. Though technically his actions did not violate any law, many found his actions objectionable. As one newspaper editor put it "the only difference between a bank burglar and the president is that one works at night." Other misdeeds were brought to light by Pecora, leading to Mitchell's resignation from the board of National City Bank and a multi-million-dollar settlement of civil charges of tax evasion.

Pecora called perhaps the biggest fish of all, J.P. Morgan, Jr., to the stand to testify. One of the senators in the hearing, Carter Glass, a Democrat from Virginia, described the scene as a "circus, and the only thing lacking now are peanuts and colored lemonade." Through skillful questioning--

Pecora was a very adroit prosecutor and good at his work--he was able to reveal that Morgan maintained a "preferred" list of high-profile clients of the bank who were offered stock at extremely favorable prices. The list included former president Calvin Coolidge and Supreme Court Justice Owen J. Roberts. Morgan also told the committee that due to his stock market losses in 1929 he had paid no taxes in 1930 through 1932. Though Morgan had committed no crimes, the publicity was damming. Morgan's testimony marked the highwater point of the hearings, with additional bankers giving testimony for the next several months.

After over two years of investigation the committee issued a massive four-hundred-page final report in June 1934. The report offered a detailed analysis of banking practices but stopped short of making specific legislative recommendations. At the urging of President Roosevelt, legislation meant to regulate banks and the market had already been established.

Spurred on by the public outcry over the abusive banking practices, Congress enacted several pieces of legislation designed to regulate banking and the stock market. In June 1933 Congress passed the Banking Act, also known as the Glass-Steagall Act, which restricted the American banking system, separating investment firms from commercial banks. To prevent runs on banks, Congress established the Federal Bank Deposit Insurance Corporation, now known as the FDIC, to guarantee deposits in individual banks.

The Start of the Securities and Exchange Commission

The Roosevelt administration pushed for more regulation of the stock market, which drew harsh criticism from the leaders of Wall Street. There was also opposition from within the Republican Party among those who believed the federal takeover of the NYSE was socialism. According to the Republican congressman Fred Britten of Illinois, "The real object of this bill is to Russianize everything worthwhile." The opposition was weak, and the Securities Exchange Act of 1934 passed into law. Gone was the independence Wall Street had enjoyed since 1791. Stock exchanges now had to register with the newly created Securities and Exchange Commission (SEC). Practices on the exchanges, including short selling and margin requirements, were standardized.

Pecora had hoped to be named the head of the SEC, but Roosevelt surprised everyone and named Joseph P. Kennedy as head of the organization. Kennedy's appointment drew harsh criticism and Roosevelt was accused of selling out to Wall Street. When President Roosevelt was asked why he chose the former stock manipulator he replied, "Takes one to catch one." Pecora became the commissioner of the SEC, answering to Kennedy. Kennedy's background as a bear market operator—one who profits when prices drop—meant he was the only member of the commission who had participated in many of the activities the new department was to regulate. Kennedy turned out to be an able administrator, setting up the mechanics of how to regulate the stock and bond exchanges and putting into place procedures to investigate bankers and brokers involved in misdeeds.

Conclusion

The stock market crash of 1929 was one of the landmark events in the twentieth century. Billions of dollars of the hard-earned savings of average Americans were erased in a few short months. The market crash was the opening chapter in the greatest financial depression the nation had faced, throwing millions into poverty. Through the dark decade of the 1930s the nation struggled to regain its footing, not climbing out of the depression until the start of World War II. The stock market crash did force the issue of regulation, which turned the stock exchanges from an "ole boys" club into a modern and efficient worldwide marketplace for securities and commodities, where both producers and investors could potentially profit.

The End

Thank you for reading my book. I hope you found it worth your time and money. Please don't forget to leave a review for this short book. I read each review and they help me become a better writer.

- Doug

Timeline of
the Stock Market Crash of 1929

January 2, 1920 – The Dow Jones Industrial Average closing price is 108.76.

March 3, 1928 – The stock of RCA is priced at $77 per share, by December 31 it is over $400.

March 4, 1929 – Herbert Hoover is inaugurated as President of the United States.

September 3, 1929 – The Dow Jones Industrial Average reaches an historic high of 381.

October 24, 1929 – Black Thursday. Stocks sell off early in the day under unusually heavy volume but recover most of the lost ground by the end of trading.

October 29, 1929 – Black Tuesday. Dow Jones Industrial Average drops nearly 12 percent to close at 230.

November 21, 1929 – President Hoover rallies business leaders to calm the markets and the general public.

November 23, 1929 – Hoover requests that governors from all forty-eight states expand public spending, keeping employment high.

June 17, 1930 – President Hoover signs Hawley-Smoot Tariff Act, raising U.S. tariffs to historic levels and instigating an international trade war.

September 9, 1930 – The State Department announces it will limit immigration until unemployment lessens.

December 11, 1930 – Bank of United States, with 60 branches in New York, closes its doors.

October 8, 1931 – The Federal Reserve Bank of New York raises the rediscount rate from 1.5 percent to 2.5 percent. A week later they raise the rate to 3.5 percent.

November 8, 1932 – Franklin D. Roosevelt, governor of New York, wins presidential election, soundly defeating Herbert Hoover.

1931-1932 – More than five thousand U.S. banks fail.

1932 – Glass-Steagall Act of 1932 becomes law. Title: "An Act to Improve the facilities of the Federal Reserve System for the Service of Commerce, Industry, & Agriculture, to Provide Means for Meeting the Needs of Member Banks in Exceptional Circumstances & for Other Purposes."

March 15, 1933 – Dow climbs 15 percent to 62, the largest one day upward move in history.

1933 – The 1933 Banking Act establishes the Federal Deposit Insurance Corporation (FDIC) and imposes various banking reforms. The Securities Act of 1933 set penalties for filing false information about stock offerings.

1934 – The Securities Act of 1934 forms the Securities and Exchange Commission to regulate the stock exchanges.

November 23, 1954 – The Dow Jones Industrial Average closes at 283.74, which is the first closing price above the September 3, 1929, high.

Biographical Sketches

<u>Baruch, Bernard</u> (1870 – 1965) was a venture capitalist, investor, and government official. Bernard Baruch was born in Camden, South Carolina, reared in New York city, and graduated from the City College of New York in 1889. His first job was on Wall Street for $3 per week; by age thirty he was a millionaire. He was the governor of the New York Stock Exchange and a leader in mining finance. During World War I President Woodrow Wilson appointed him as chairman of the War Industries Board, which gave him sweeping powers over the U.S. economy. After the war he served in a senior capacity with the U.S. peace delegation at the Treaty of Versailles that ended World War I. Though he did not completely exit the stock market before the 1929 crash, it is reported that he was able to limit his losses and retain much of his fortune. At age seventy-five, President Harry Truman named Baruch to present to the United

Nations the U.S. plan for the international control of atomic energy.

Durant, William C. (1861 – 1947) was a leader in the automotive industry, co-founder of both General Motors and Chevrolet, and a Wall Street speculator during the 1920s. William Durant was born in Boston, Massachusetts, but grew up in his grandfather's house in Flint, Michigan. In 1885 he went into business manufacturing and selling carriages, switching to the automobile business in 1904. During his long career as an auto manufacturer he either was the head or had a significant ownership in the Buick Motor Car Company, General Motors Company, Chevrolet Motor Car Company, and others. In the economic downturn of 1920, the stock of General Motors declined sharply, Durant made large purchases of the stock on margin. He quickly became overextended as the stock price dropped, resulting in his resignation as president of General Motors in December 1920. During the 1920s he was a stock market speculator and founded Durant Motors. The car company was unsuccessful, and he filed for bankruptcy in 1935, listing liabilities of $914,000 and assets of $250. In his seventies, he returned to Flint, Michigan, and launched a chain of bowling alleys. Durant was known for his warm and likable personality.

Hoover, Herbert (1874 – 1964) was a successful mining engineer, humanitarian, Secretary of Commerce, and the thirty-first president of the United States. Herbert Hoover was born into a modest Quaker family in West Branch, Iowa. He was orphaned at age nine and went to live with his uncle in Oregon. After graduating from Stanford University, he worked various jobs then joined the British mining company of Berwik, Moering. As an engineer he worked for the company in China and Australia. He married his college sweetheart, Lou Henry, and they had two children. During World War I Hoover led an effort to arrange safe passage for thousands of American stranded in Europe and organized the Belgium relief effort that fed millions. Under

Presidents Harding and Coolidge, he was a highly effective Secretary of Commerce. His notoriety from his humanitarian efforts and his successful leadership in the government resulted in a landslide victory in the presidential election of 1928. After the stock market crash in 1929 and the start of the Great Depression, Hoover spent much of his time as president attempting to resurrect the failing economy. Hoover promoted cooperative private-sector and government relief efforts to aid the slumping agricultural sector. The growing depression brought on a move to the Democratic party by many voters, bringing about a significant loss for Hoover in the presidential election of 1932. After the presidency, he was active in Republican politics and in debates concerning President Roosevelt's New Deal policies. During World War II he headed a European food relief effort at the request of President Harry Truman.

Figure – President Herbert Hoover.

<u>Kennedy, Joseph P.</u> (1888 – 1969) was a prominent financier and government official. Born in Boston to a family of modest means, Joseph Kennedy graduated from Harvard in 1912 and two years later became president of Columbia Trust Company. After World War I he was heavily engaged in stock market speculation leading up to the 1929 stock market crash. He also was involved in the motion-picture business, owning several movie theaters and arranging the

merger that created RKO Pictures. By the 1930s he was a millionaire many times over, and later in the decade he was involved in the administration of President Franklin Roosevelt. Kennedy became the first chairman of the newly formed Securities and Exchange Commission (SEC) in 1935. As a previous stock market speculator, his appointment as a regulator of the stock market shocked many, including the Secretary of the Interior Harold L. Ickes. During the Roosevelt administration he served as the chairman of the United States Maritime Commission and then the ambassador to Great Britain.

Kennedy married Rose Fitzgerald in 1914 and together they would have eight children. Three of their sons became famous politicians: John F. Kennedy, 35th President of the United States; Robert F. Kennedy, U.S. Attorney General and Senator from New York; and Edward M. Kennedy, Senator from Massachusetts.

<u>Lamont, Thomas W.</u> (1870 -1948) was an American financier. Thomas Lamont was born in Claverack, New York. He was the son of a rural Methodist minister and graduated from Harvard University in 1892. After becoming a reporter for the *New York Tribune*, starting his own business, he became a banker. In 1911 he became a partner at the firm of J.P. Morgan and Company. During World War I he joined the Liberty Loan Committee to sell war bonds to Americans. At the end of the war he was appointed as a representative to the Paris Peace Conference, drawing up plans to set reparation payments for Germany. He was a member of the Council of Foreign Relations and unofficial advisor to Presidents Wilson, Hoover, and Roosevelt. Days before the October 1929 stock market crash, President Hoover contacted Lamont about the rampant speculation in the stock market. Lamont assured the president there was no cause for alarm, saying, "The future appears brilliant." During the stock market crash Lamont organized Wall Street firms to purchase large blocks of

stock to end the price slide. Their efforts failed, and the stock market lost one quarter of its value that week. In 1943, J.P. Morgan & Company reorganized, and Lamont became chairman of the board of directors. He was active in charities, donating funding for the Lamont Library at Harvard University.

Mitchell, Charles E. (1877 – 1955) was the head of First National Bank (now Citibank) for 12 years during the first half of the twentieth century. In this position his reckless stock promotion contributed to the stock market crash of 1929. Charles Mitchell was born in Chelsea, Massachusetts, and graduated from Amherst College in 1899. After graduation he worked for the Western Electric Company in Chicago. From there he moved to New York City, working in banking and investments. In 1921 he was elected president of National City Bank and the bank's subsidiary National City Company. Under his leadership the bank expanded rapidly, and the National City Company became the world's largest security issuing entity. His salesmen sold millions of shares of the bank's stock, which fell drastically during the market crash of 1929. Mitchell was arrested in 1933 and indicted for tax evasion. He was found not guilty of criminal activity, but the government won a $1 million civil settlement against him. In 1933 he was called before the Senate's Pecora Commission, which investigated Mitchell for his sale in the loss of millions of dollars in the market crash, excessive pay, and tax avoidance. Disgraced, he left National City. Later in his life he made a comeback to become a successful Wall Street banker.

Pecora, Ferdinand (1882 -1971) was an American lawyer and New York State Supreme Court judge. Ferdinand Pecora was born in Nicosia, Sicily, and emigrated with his parents to the United States in 1886. Forced to leave school early he found work as clerk in a Wall Street firm. He attended New York Law School and was admitted to the New York bar in 1911. In 1918, he was appointed as an assistant district attorney in New York City. There he earned a reputation as a talented and honest prosecutor. During the U.S. Senate's Committee on Banking and Currency hearings in January 1933, he was appointed Chief Counsel. During the senate committee hearings, led by Pecora, many of the leading bankers were brought before the senators, exposing much of the corruption that led to the 1929 stock market crash. Out of the hearings came a string of legislation to regulate the banking industry and the stock market. After the hearings, Pecora was appointed a commissioner of the newly formed Securities and Exchange Commission (SEC). He left the SEC in less than a year and became a judge of the New York Supreme Court, a position he held until 1950.

References and Further Reading

Bierman, Harold. "The 1929 Stock Market Crash." EH.Net Encyclopedia, edited by Robert Whaples. Accessed May 27, 2020. URL https://eh.net/encyclopedia/the-1929-stock-market-crash/

Boyer, Paul S. (Editor) *The Oxford Companion to United States History*. Oxford University Press. 2001.

Daniel, Clifton (Editor in Chief) *20th Century Day by Day*. Dorling Kindersley Limited, London. 2000.

Garraty, John A. and Mark C. Carnes (Editors). *Dictionary of American Biography*. Supplement Eight 1966-1970. Charles Scribner's Sons. 1988.

Geisst, Charles R. *Wall Street: A History*. Updated Edition. Oxford University Press. 1997.

King, Gilbert. "The Man Who Busted the 'Banksters.' " smithsonianmag.com, November

29, 2011. Accessed May 21, 2020. URL https://www.smithsonianmag.com/history/the-man-who-busted-the-banksters-932416/

Klein, Maury. *Rainbow's End: The Crash of 1929*. Oxford University Press. 2001.

Reeves, T. C. *Twentieth-Century America: A Brief History*. Oxford University Press. 2000.

Shales, Amity. *The Forgotten Man: A New History of the Great Depression*. Harper Perennial. 2007.

Thomas, Gordon and Max Morgan-Witts. *The Day the Bubble Burst: A Social History of the Wall Street Crash of 1929*. Penguin Books. 1980.

Watkins, T.H. *The Hungry Years: A Narrative History of the Great Depression in America*. Henry Holt and Company, LLC. 1999.

West, Doug. *Herbert Hoover: A Short Biography: Thirty-First President of the United States*. C&D Publications. 2020.

Williamson, Samuel H. "Daily Closing Value of the Dow Jones Average, 1885 to Present." MeasuringWorth, 2020. Accessed May 18, 2020. URL https://www.measuringworth.com/datasets/DJA/index.php

Subcommittee on Senate Resolutions 84 and 239 (The Pecora Committee), Notable Senate Investigations, U.S. Senate Historical Office, Washington, D.C.

Acknowledgements

I would like to thank Cynthia West and Lisa Zahn for her help in preparation of this book. All the photographs are from the public domain.

About the Author

Figure – Doug West
(photo by Karina West)

Doug West is a retired engineer, small business owner, and experienced writer with several books to his credit. His writing interests are general, with expertise in science, history, and biographies. Doug has a B.S. in Physics from the Missouri School of Science and Technology and a Ph.D. in General Engineering from Oklahoma State University. He lives with his wife and little dog "Millie" near Kansas City, Missouri. Additional books by Doug West can be found at https://www.amazon.com/Doug-West/e/B00961PJ8M. Follow the author on Facebook at:
https://www.facebook.com/30minutebooks.

Additional Books by Doug West

Buying and Selling Silver Bullion Like a Pro

How to Write, Publish, and Market Your Own Audio Book

A Short Biography of the Scientist Sir Isaac Newton

A Short Biography of the Astronomer Edwin Hubble

Galileo Galilei – A Short Biography

Benjamin Franklin – A Short Biography

The Astronomer Cecilia Payne-Gaposchkin – A Short Biography

The American Revolutionary War – A Short History

Coinage of the United States – A Short History

John Adams – A Short Biography

In the Footsteps of Columbus (Annotated) Introduction and Biography Included (with Annie J. Cannon)

Alexander Hamilton – Illustrated and Annotated (with Charles A. Conant)

Harlow Shapley – Biography of an Astronomer

Alexander Hamilton – A Short Biography

The Great Depression – A Short History

Jesse Owens, Adolf Hitler and the 1936 Summer Olympics

Thomas Jefferson – A Short Biography

Gold of My Father – A Short Tale of Adventure

Making Your Money Grow with Dividend Paying Stocks – Revised Edition

The French and Indian War – A Short History

The Mathematician John Forbes Nash Jr. – A Short Biography

The British Prime Minister Margaret Thatcher – A Short Biography

Vice President Mike Pence – A Short Biography

President Jimmy Carter – A Short Biography

President Ronald Reagan – A Short Biography

President George H. W. Bush – A Short Biography

Dr. Robert H. Goddard – A Brief Biography - Father of American Rocketry and the Space Age

Richard Nixon: A Short Biography - 37th President of the United States

Charles Lindbergh: A Short Biography - Famed Aviator and Environmentalist

Dr. Wernher von Braun: A Short Biography - Pioneer of Rocketry and Space Exploration

Bill Clinton: A Short Biography – 42nd President of the United States

Joe Biden: A Short Biography - 47th Vice President of the United States

Donald Trump: A Short Biography - 45th President of the United States

Nicolaus Copernicus: A Short Biography - The Astronomer Who Moved the Earth

America's Second War of Independence: A Short History of the War of 1812

John Quincy Adams: A Short Biography - Sixth President of the United States

Andrew Jackson: A Short Biography: Seventh President of the United States

Albert Einstein: A Short Biography Father of the Theory of Relativity

Franklin Delano Roosevelt: A Short Biography: Thirty-Second President of the United States

James Clerk Maxwell: A Short Biography: Giant of Nineteenth-Century Physics

Ernest Rutherford: A Short Biography: The Father of Nuclear Physics

Sir William Crookes: A Short Biography: Nineteenth-Century British Chemist and Spiritualist

The Journey of Apollo 11 to the Moon

William Henry Harrison: A Short Biography: Tenth President of the United States

John Tyler: A Short Biography: Eleventh President of the United States

James K. Polk: A Short Biography: Eleventh President of the United States

Louisa Catherine Adams: A Short Biography: First Lady of the United States

Samuel Adams: A Short Biography: Architect of the American Revolution

The Mexican-American War: A Short History: America's Fulfillment of Manifest Destiny

History of the Plymouth and Massachusetts Bay Colonies: Pilgrims, Puritans, and the Founding of New England

The History of the Jamestown Colony: America's First Permanent English Settlement

Zachary Taylor: A Short Biography: Twelfth President of the United States

Herbert Hoover: A Short Biography: Thirty-First President of the United States

Index

www.ingramcontent.com/pod-product-compliance
Lightning Source LLC
Chambersburg PA
CBHW020558220526
45463CB00006B/2355

9798656419765